About the Author

D J Melville is a natural author and storyteller, outdoorsman, teacher and lover of nature. In this charming book, he recalls all his most significant encounters with the natural world and its wildlife. In so doing, he lays a foundation for an interest in the conservation of our natural heritage in current and future generations. He also shows us how important it is to be aware of all the natural life that surrounds us every day, whether we live in an urban or rural environment.

I would recommend this book to influence parents, teachers and those who work with young people. Furthermore, as compulsory reading in schools, to teach the children or students at their most impressionable age how important and beautiful nature is to all of us here on Earth.

Photo credit: Harpreet Kaur, MagentaPhotography.com

Natural History Encounters

D J Melville

Natural History Encounters

Artwork cover and stoat drawing by Carolyn Cox,
inside illustrations by Rubi Hussey.

Olympia Publishers
London

www.olympiapublishers.com
OLYMPIA PAPERBACK EDITION

A CIP catalogue record for this title is
available from the British Library.

ISBN: 978-1-80074-364-9

This is a work of creative nonfiction. The events are portrayed to the
best of the author's memory. While all the stories in this book are
true, some names and identifying details have been changed to
protect the privacy of the people involved.

First Published in 2023

Olympia Publishers
Tallis House
2 Tallis Street
London
EC4Y 0AB

Printed in Great Britain

Dedication

This book is dedicated to my late parents with thanks for their encouragement. To Jim and 'Mima' Melville plus Aunty Jean Storey (both née Saulters).

Also, to Eloise Isabella, my first granddaughter, and future generations.

Acknowledgements

I would like to thank Shirley Darlington especially for the initial editing but also for the encouragement and enthusiasm from the inception of an idea. Ian and Mary Hempshall for doing an overview and proof reading respectively—a friendly yet expertly done first read with a sympathetic yet professional input. To Rubi Hussey, the very gifted illustrator, on her perfect interpretations and to Carolyn Cox for the contemporary linocut cover inspiration, capturing beautifully the most important stoat moment. Special thanks also to Margaret Sweatman, the amateur photographer who took the photo of the chimps in Rwanda from which Rubi based her drawing. Rachel Ledbetter, Barnabus Books, LLC, Alexandria, Virginia, USA who from the first zoom meet, believed in the book and has since prayed for it. The wider Creation Care team at Trinity Church, Lewes, including Rob and Jan Hoy who did the final read, plus A Rocha friends and former colleagues who have been part of the journey. Appreciation to the publication team at Olympia — James Houghton and Kristina Smith — my main contacts for providing this opportunity. To all other organisations that have enabled me to learn and indulge in my passion — sometimes inadvertently — and the many individuals in those organisations who will know who they are. And lastly, my thanks go to my wife, Annette, who has been a solid companion and encourager, who came into my life and brought her two daughters, Nicole and Corrine, with her. They, with Emma, my daughter, are drawn in the last illustration — Thanks all.

Natural History Encounters — Foreword

Natural History Encounters is a smorgasbord of the author's experiences from primary school awakenings in Northern Ireland, then college in Scotland, to living in later life in the south of England. While geography and recording technology may change, the common threads are close encounters and observations of the natural world. The book is divided into five main sections: Awakenings, Arrivals, Awareness, Acceptance and Au revoir totalling twenty short stories with a poem — by the author and guests — to start each part.

Awakenings covers the author's impressionable years at Crumlin Primary School, where drawing and tracing birds was a major preoccupation. The first poem and story embrace the early freedoms the previous generation had. Parents actively encouraged you to pack nothing but a Kodak instamatic camera (black and white film in those days) and to walk miles, recording spring alone in the countryside; something perhaps unthinkable and reckless today. The transition of moving countries is also included in this part which, while daunting, has much to celebrate in natural history terms—I had never seen a woodpecker before, but I did miss the curlews. This section finishes with stimulating encounters experienced in a tropical country.

Arrivals covers a different transition where the business of life — marriage, familial priorities, and divorce — unfolds leading to the real solace that nature and faith can provide. A new contentment is the result, and these short stories include wonderful holiday and sabbatical moments for the author to savour wild places when alone or in community with others.

Awareness includes encounters working with children — both primary school and secondary students — in nature's classroom. Jocular moments are recalled of incidents where we all learnt.

Acceptance comes when living on a farm in the South Downs for nearly thirty years, and these close encounters are at the heart of the book. This gave me an entitlement to stride out on my own patch whether to record for the BTO Bird Atlas 2011/2015 or just for good exercise which benefits health. What is recorded here are the unexpected encounters with wildlife which can be shared on social media. In fact, the modern era means that it is easier than ever with a phone camera in the pocket to photograph, research and record. However, there is a challenge when it is all at your fingertips to settle in a chair and enjoy the pixelated version. If this book does nothing else but gets you out of your chair to experience nature in its full sensory 3D version, I will have succeeded. As I said in one of the very short stories in this section, if you come across a close-up of a stoat or fox in the wild it is a moment to drop everything, including the camera, and savour.

In Au revoir, I say goodbye to my old home village with family in a spectacular encounter. Then I veer into the mystery genre in what is a true story, reminding us all that not everything is explainable. The modern era also ends with a pleasurable visit to Jamaica.

David Melville, Lewes, October 2020.

Part 1 Awakenings —

Early encounters, that influenced change, from childhood in County Antrim, to living in Kent and Sri Lanka in the 1980s.

1
First time

Call it nostalgia,
I call it bliss,
to revisit the moment
that inspired me to exist.

An Ulster country lane,
full of hedges, gorse and haw,
where a female blackbird sat,
as I recorded her, the spring raw.

Now in the Autumn,
40 years have passed,
that moment was so special,
for the intervening life amassed.

Created for an RSPB competition on early magical natural
moments (never published)

October 2008

2
Impressionable years — Corncrakes and Curlews

Every generation will connect with the natural world in their own way. What is becoming increasingly obvious — due to the rapid changes in the last hundred years — is that within a few generations the experiences have been very different. I can only record my own. Growing up in Ulster in the 1960s and 1970s was special, due to the adventures we had connecting to the rural environment, which, after all, is the purpose of this book. These early experiences shape you, as we are all products of our impressionable years. I now share a few with you, to enable you to understand my bedrock, setting the scene for the rest of the book.

My mother was a Saulters, and the family homestead was affectionately known as 'Ballydownfine'. Though a Belfast address, it was really on the outskirts of Upper Springfield Road and was nestled in the lee of the Black Mountain, part of which is a National Trust area. As my mum was one of nine children (four sisters, four brothers; one or two Alsatian dogs), by the time the cousins came along it was a playground for us. My grandfather was a civil servant but kept a smallholding of a few acres to supplement his income. At one time it was a real menagerie with pigs, a cow or two, and a goat but I only remember the poultry: ducks who had a small duck-pond and hens who had a run — there was also an orchard. The geese were the best guards, as they would announce your arrival with lots of honking and territorial neck stretching. They meant business and 'Old Barney' the gander would nip your ankles given half a chance. Even the matriarch of our family — my grandmother — was not exempt from his attention, whilst being frail and less mobile in her older years. The gander would take the opportunity as people tried to get from the car by hopping, skipping and jumping to the back porch.

Occasionally a dull orange beak with a serrated edge would meet soft, exposed flesh. As Christmas loomed, to meet the demands of such a big family's food festivity, each year a goose and a turkey met their demise. My grandfather would select the plumpest, then with the help of my uncles and aunties, they would humanely kill it on site before plucking and gutting followed by final preparations. I think everyone understood exactly where their Christmas meal came from, Local, Organic, Animal-friendly and Fairly traded (to use the LOAF criteria).

We were aware that swallows flew low in the yard as they nested in the outhouses with many exit and entry points. Cuckoos could also be heard regularly in the valley. Having a sleepover for a child for the first time is always an anxious experience but this place had the added distraction of a corncrake *Crex crex* going *kerrx kerrx* all night long. How times have changed, as the location was on the mountain spring line, above the city and they still had hayfields beside this smallholding. Today you would have to travel as far north as Rathlin Island or as far west as Donegal to hear them, though they have confirmed breeders in County Down, to the south too.

When my mother married a 'Crumlin man', she moved fourteen miles away to that village, but there was a sister, who married a farmer three miles away up the road and the Harknesses lived on a farm called 'Fourscore'. It was called this after the national school which was adjacent to their largest field of eighty acres (or 4 score = 4 x 20) and had an ancient fort or two as well as the beautiful natural Glenavy River as the boundary. My uncle let most of the land out, worked as a butcher in the city and had a passion for pigeon racing. He eventually received the highest accolade by winning the 'Irish Young Bird National' in 1971, with Black Prince who flew the quickest from Penzance 310 miles away. In addition to the proud status for this achievement, he won a huge colour TV, the first that neighbours — friends and family — had seen! Importantly we had five cousins — four boys and the oldest a girl — who lived there, so it was a treasure trove of holiday entertainment and natural education for my brother and me. These were halcyon days staying over on holiday in the formidable farmhouse of black and pale-yellow cornerstones — two floors high plus an attic. The challenge was getting there as we didn't have a car then, there was no direct bus service, but we had one children's bike between my brother and me. So not to be deterred, my Mum would encourage us to ride the bike as far as the eye could see, before setting the bike in the long grass for the other to take over; she, of course, walked the lot. Once we got there it was all worth it, the arduous journey soon forgotten, we quickly set off on our expeditions down the fields as six boys and one or two dogs. These experiences were formative in so many fun ways. Interestingly one cousin got his leg pulled, when we found a stick which said his name on it, with Sargent preceding it, around the fort area. He had the last laugh as he ended up in the Irish Guards, Chelsea Barracks in London! The river was a great attraction and though officially I learnt to swim doing the breaststroke in Portrush Harbour with an instructor, unofficially it was wild swimming, doing the doggie paddle with the dogs and my cousins. It was after all the best way to keep any 'cleggs' (horse flies) at bay. Our older girl cousin did not join us on many of these trips, but years later told us she had the job of keeping a watch on us, using binoculars from the second floor. I do hope she was spared the sight of us all skinny dipping, by the trees on the riverbank. Throughout our time growing up in holidays at 'fourscore' there was the sound of curlews *Numenius arquata* and while a background part of the ambience, I am sure they were breeding there at that time amongst the damp pasture of tussock grass and compact rush. Other memorable moments to record were that my uncle enjoyed playing the Lambeg Drum and bred female goats for the skins to completely cover this one of the largest and loudest of drums. The rumour that was perpetuated by us immature boys was that male goatskins would not cover it due to the natural hole for the penis! In reality, since the spine of the goat skin covered the middle of the drum, female goats were more likely preferred due to their more rapid growth and absence of battle scars. It was a shock for us children to see a goat shortly after it was killed and skinned hanging in a barn while still warm. There was even a crocodile or alligator skin hanging in another barn. It was shrouded in mystery from whence it came and its whereabouts, to where it had gone. While at early secondary school age, I also first experienced hunting for rabbits and fish with my older boy cousin. It was a turning point in that after shooting a stationary rabbit, I decided I would much rather capture them using a camera. This close cousin was also an ace fisherperson and had a local record of twenty-four brown trout, in one day during the flood season, teaching my brother and me to fish in the process.

The adventures continued as we would join these same cousins (and others), around the Northern Irish coast, in such stunning settings as Annalong and Ballywalter, County Down, in the shadow of the Mourne Mountains. We even had access to our own rowing boat. The cry would go out as we crossed the bay usually with one lagging behind doing the doggie paddle: "Ahoy there ye land lubbers"

Our family holidays tended to be on the north Antrim coastline near Portrush where the north Atlantic crashed into sandy beaches. No wet suits for us then, but at Easter after swimming it felt so cold that hypothermia was never far away if you didn't change quickly. Being more into the minutiae of things, than the scenery, we enjoyed rock pooling for shore crabs and minnows in jam jars, occasionally coming across a black rectangular mermaid's purse (ray or skate embryonic pouch). Once when sea fishing with my family, with gannets dive bombing as a backdrop, I maintain to this day that I saw a huge fin. It was too big to be a shark so it must have been an 'orca', a killer whale. Unfortunately, no one else (including myself) saw it again.

My father also influenced us by readily finding lots of birds' nests. A lapwing nest he found in the Glens of Antrim was really impressive, as it was so beautiful, camouflaged and is profound in my memory. Years later as an adult I respect how difficult it was to locate these nests in my failed attempts to record them for the British Trust for Ornithology. So, respect for his detective nest skills, even though there were probably more around then. Back in Crumlin, he found nests in the hedgerows on quiet country ambles around the village. It must have run in the family, as my dad's younger brother migrated to Hayes, in west London. A welder by trade, he bred canaries in the back garden as a passion, eventually becoming a national judge. Nearing the end of my primary school years, when I was aged eleven, my parents would encourage me to enjoy spring field trips. This is where I could experience solitude doing a circular walk down Cidercourt Road, along by Tom Hen Tots — as it was colloquially named — and back up the Lurgan Road with stunning views over Rams Island in Lough Neagh, the largest freshwater lough in the UK and the rest of Ireland. I must have been acquiring my own skills of early nest detection, as a photograph from that era, of a blackbird sitting on the nest proves, albeit well concealed.

During the secondary school years with the onset of puberty there were plenty of other worthy distractions from engaging with the natural world but the first job I loved was farm summer holiday harvesting of hay and straw. This later materialised into Saturday work on a dairy farm and eventually helping with cattle shows for pedigree Ayrshires. School geography field trips plus increasingly camping holidays without parents to the Isle of Arran were also exciting and provided more independent encounters.

We all have our own stories of places and the adults who inspire us along the way. I hope you will see in this book that the generations may change but the constant is the connection with the natural world. My hope is that you will help influence the next generation to care for nature and wildlife in a way that is becoming increasingly important for our mutual coexistence.

3
Suffering in a beautiful setting

Spare a thought as you sit snug in your living room, in front of a blazing fire, for some of our feathered friends who are not so fortunate. Winter on the pond at the Old Mill, Tonge, near Sittingbourne in Kent, must prove a very cold experience for the ducks, which, for some reason, choose not to fly south. While out walking one Sunday, this chilling fact was brought home. On entering the gates, I was confronted by the usual barrage of tufted, mallard and teal—only to discover I had forgotten the bread again.

However, this time the atmosphere was slightly different. There was a sense of urgency or hunger since, on such a cold day, tourists are not in evidence.

Perhaps the most striking thing was that one large white drake appeared to have been frozen by the breast feathers to the ice, about two metres from the nearest bank. With both feet sliding aimlessly at its side, it was indeed a pitiful sight.

As the sun lowered, the light and temperature were fading fast. Ironically, in this beautiful setting, a slow, agonising death was in store for this creature.

A few people had gathered showing equal concern regardless of their different backgrounds. Could it be towed with a rope, lassoed ashore or lured with bread? Would it even be possible to break the ice by using some driftwood in the immediate area without damage to the bird?

It was by trying this last ploy that we discovered by nearly clobbering the stranded drake, that it was in fact injured. Therefore, it was not capable of rising to its feet.

A decision was taken to telephone the RSPCA. They promptly arrived and in a more professional manner which had been so far lacking, captured the wounded creature to make a thorough investigation in a warmer environment.

Slowly we returned to our own habitats brought together by a common bond to rescue a helpless animal. Thoughts turned back to the snug sitting room with its blazing fire. The sun lowered further on this winter scene with its potentially dire consequences.

Published letter in the *Sittingbourne News*, part of *Kent Messenger* — circa winter 1985.
Original was typed on a typewriter.

4
Ayubowan — May you live a thousand years

My ex-wife, who was also northern Irish, had recently moved to England. We wished to fulfil an ambition, that we could experience living in a tropical country for a while, for mutual benefit. On Easter Saturday April 1988, we boarded the overnight Tristar, with the blessings of family and friends from Sittingbourne United Reformed Church still ringing in our ears, and woke up in Colombo, Sri Lanka.

The door of the aircraft opened, and it felt like we had just opened the oven door! This was going to be different, despite a year's preparation by Voluntary Services Overseas and the Overseas Development Natural Resources Institute (now NRI). First impressions were a total assault on the senses like stepping into a tropical natural history programme but with additional stimulus overload of smells and sounds. Taste would come later when introduced to rice and curry followed by buffalo curd, pineapple with jaggery—sweet sugar cane and palm sap. I remember saying to a work colleague during the induction, "Do you have, really large bats in this country?" "No just normal size" he replied, which to him was the 60 cm wingspan of the fruit bat. I guess it is all relative as normal to us is the pipistrelle with a wingspan of 20 cm; their bats are bigger than our crows! After language tuition in the beautiful setting of Colombo's YWCA for the urban acclimatisation, we were off for the weekend to a village called Ganemula to sample country village life. I was fascinated by the green vegetation of tropical fruit and nuts, the humid conditions and spectacular thunderstorms of the monsoon season. People were by necessity living cheek by jowl with ants, mosquitoes, spiders, and rats but also had indoor geckos, sunbirds, kingfishers, pelicans and storks.

By now I was looking forward to our time in this the Isle of Serendip even as a foreign *Sudu Mahaththeya* (white Mister). It had such a mix of cultures: Buddhist, Hindu, Muslim and Christian (mostly Catholic) and the former influences of the Independent Kandayan Kings, the Portuguese, Dutch and British colonisers. The two main ethnic groups of Tamil and Sinhalese have been well documented due to the past strife but like many countries there are also mixed heritage people. In Sri Lanka they are called Burghers — historically the offspring from the Dutch and Ceylonese, Ceylon being the name of the island before independence.

We had settled into our new home beside the paddy fields with the address of Kirimandala Mawatha (Milk Board Road!). Cows in the Hill Country of Nuwara Eliya provided milk for the city and had a depot in this area of Colombo. We were ready to embark on our work; for my ex-wife, Community Health Work and for me, Coconut Fibre Processing. The house we initially stayed in was frugal but ample (no air conditioning and overhead fans), but it did have a natural recycling system. Thankfully there was little plastic packaging, the compost waste we were told to just throw down the back of the garden and the heat plus nature in the tropics would do the rest. Imagine my surprise the next morning to see a 'lounge' of three monitor lizards — 2–3 metres from nose to tail — feasting on the scraps. I quickly grabbed a camera, pulled on a sarong and a pair of flip-flops before slowly approaching the lizards who had stopped mid-bite to look back at me suspiciously. After I got my photo there was a bit of stand-off, as we eyed each other up. I turned to retreat slowly when suddenly splat! my flip-flop noisily came out of the sticky ground! I heard a scurrying behind me and bolted, not knowing which direction the monitor lizard was coming from or going to.

I was now having regular visits to the coconut triangle of Kurunegala, north of Colombo in a place called Lunuwila which also had a Coconut Research Institute rest house for overnight stays. I was blown away by the beauty of the plantations and the water tanks with lotus flowers, initially riding by motorbike en route to work where Indian rollers and woodpeckers could be seen in the trees. Snakes are abundant and there are 96 different species (50 endemics on the island), many are venomous. As a general rule, the smaller the snake the more deadly, so it pays to make some noise and ground vibration in long grass, rather than sneaking about quietly. I did witness a violent reaction to a cobra being discovered by the mill workers at the cooperative I was working at, when they extinguished it rapidly, with long sticks in a team effort. Workers were barefooted and wore a loincloth so perceived it as a threat. In the same area at the Nattandiya Sawmills, working Asian elephants *Elephas maximus* were lifting a few logs which had been chained together, then joined to a large ball like chewing gum, which the elephant puts in its mouth.

By straining their neck muscles, they lifted the tree logs clear of the ground before transporting them to another place. One weekend my ex-wife joined me out-station and on a visit to the sawmill we were asked if we would like to ride on the elephant's back. The hairs on its neck and upper back are quite coarse and when the Mahout saw that my ex-wife and I had only light cotton garments on, he immediately found a jute bag which was quickly dusted down and thrown over the elephant's shoulders for our comfort. When on the elephants back it felt like you were Hannibal, riding majestically around the height of the coconut palms. You can also understand why it is such a good vantage point for seeing tigers in India. Huge tusker elephants are also seen decorated elaborately for the Kandayan Esala Perahera—a Buddhist festival of the tooth to pay homage to a relic of the Buddha's tooth which is housed in a temple. You could get really close to elephants even in urban areas like Colombo and appreciate how well trained they could be, as they lift their huge feet and set them down gently. Each elephant has a trainer who bonds with them and also washes them in the river. He disciplines them with a stick that has a sharp barb on it.

An ambition to scuba dive was fulfilled during a vacation while based in Sri Lanka. While Sri Lanka has some coral reefs, those I saw were not in good shape because of bleaching. Atolls in the Maldives in the Indian Ocean were only a plane hop away though. Time was of the essence on this trip of a few brief days but when my German instructress suggested going down for basic PADI training straight after lunch it chimed with all the outdoor swimming advice I had been taught growing up in Northern Ireland. It would be difficult to have stomach cramps when you are moving so slowly. Nothing can prepare you for the weightless feeling on that maiden swim, when you kick the flippers and due to the buoyancy settings of your equipment — a weighted belt — you just glide halfway between the surface and the bottom one metre down. The nearest thing to being weightless would be a visit to space or the simulation of it. The author of the *Space Odyssey* series and *The View from Serendip*, Arthur C. Clarke said as much. He was an adopted resident of Sri Lanka where we met him and coincidentally were members of the same local Colombo Swimming Club. I did keep my lunch down and had beginner's luck since on that first swim I saw a moray eel, teeth and all. Later when I had gained confidence, from being in what is quite an alien environment — communication was done by sign language and by drawing on a white tile — I was also fortunate to see a triggerfish and a lionfish. When I did eventually descend just a few metres, it felt so very deep as the light quickly receded. I was fortuitous to see a large grouper fish in a small cave entrance, who defensively came out towards us before backing away. Looking down into the deep there was always that feeling that anything shark-like could appear rapidly and you were in its territory. We are so slow moving in comparison and risking the bends (DCS) if you ascended too rapidly. This brought on a mellow contemplative feeling which I found very pleasant. The final highlight on this dive was looking up at where there was a gap in the coral and a silvery shoal were just going round and around with the sun beaming down on them. So beautiful, these memories have stayed with me for well over thirty years.

Our trip of a lifetime was entering into its second phase when our daughter was born on an auspicious full moon

'Poya' Buddhist festival day. We always knew this home was temporary, but nevertheless we stayed throughout the strife of ethnic conflicts and the morning our daughter was born, we had a curfew pass to get to the hospital. This coincided with moving into a more comfortable flat which included a second-floor balcony with beautiful trees full of squirrels, coucals calling and raucous, overzealous house crows. As we neared the end of what for me was a fascinating chapter and when the baby was eight months old, it was time for one last safari to Yala National Park, in the southeast near Hambantota. This meant a very early start from Colombo by saloon car, before transferring to a jeep, to travel past the salt marshes and dead trees with elephant rock as a backdrop. We were poised for seeing the early birds which were quite impressive: the chestnut-headed bee-eaters, all hunting bees and lining up together. The crocodiles were just lying like logs — part of their ambush ploy to the unsuspecting no doubt but too far away to be any real interest to us. Suddenly our driver diverted, as he had seen a wild elephant walking in our general direction. He parked the jeep in a convenient place to observe the elephant's daily walk. We had seen many tamed elephants close up and this was no tusker (large male), but this was wild and therefore more unpredictable. We naturally watched in silence as the driver, my then wife, our new baby and I revelled in the closeness of the encounter. I was holding my breath and quietly exhaled as it walked away from us, while my daughter who had maintained silence until then just said, "Oooh," perfectly summing up the moment, while we all laughed.

My name in Sinhalese and Sanskrit. Magaa nama David Melville ඩේවිඩ් මෙල්විල් .

Postscript. Natural encounters were not at the top of my list for going to live in Sri Lanka as a new couple for the next few years. However, it wove its way into the daily fabric of my life there and the die was cast which would lead to future career changes, such was its impact. I am grateful to this country for its challenges, reshaping my worldview and eventually moving me to work influencing people about the environment and development. I am also appreciative that Karen, my ex-wife and I shared this experience, including bringing back a bonny baby girl.

Part 2 Arrivals —

Encounters around these Isles including the South Downs, Hampshire, Dorset, Arran and Rathlin, in the 1990s and early 2000s.

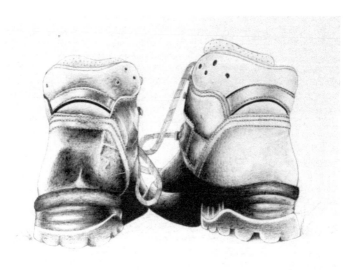

5
Human behest, nature's best

O contours of the southern Downs,
your beauty confounds.

Since where is all the cover
trees, hedges or even ragged mounds?

Like shaven brows, your rotund hills,
stand stark, naked, bare yet fair.

So majestic, so calm, life's balm,
despite human imprint, a lack of natural charm.

6
The Beauty of the Earth — The New Forest, Hampshire

I set out early for a few days' walking from the picturesque village of Burley in pursuit of the elusive ancient woodland habitat and associated wildlife. The weather is sunny with a cool breeze and a few showers forecast, perfect. A forest foal reflects my mood as it lies in the sun before rolling on its back and kicking its feet in the air. I am reminded of signs that warn these are wild animals that can kick or bite; do not get between foal and mare! These beautiful chestnut-brown ponies have owners whose initials are branded on them somewhere, as this is now common land with rights decided by a panel in Lyndhurst. Things have changed since William the Conqueror used it as a Royal hunting ground in 1079.

Through gravel forest paths of coniferous enclosures, I travel. This habitat of plantations seems a bit uniform and sterile with rows of spruce for harvesting by the Forestry Commission as a sustainable enterprise. High in the trees there is an incessant chirping as young goldcrest, blue, coal and great tits demand to be fed. A lonesome buzzard flies slowly but directly past in search of larger prey.

Deeper in the forest I leave the gravel and follow a single grass route according to my Ordnance Survey map. I discover fresh tracks and droppings of fallow deer *Dama dama* and within two minutes my anticipation has been confirmed as a small herd graze nonchalantly in a clearing. Through binoculars I enjoy the dappled sunlight bouncing off the speckled coats of a buck (stag), two does and a fawn. The buck looks at me, its sensitive nose twitching but at this distance they are content to slowly walk away grazing and displaying switching tails with a distinctive black-and-white rump.

After a few hours of walking, I reach a deciduous woodland called Mark Ash where oak, sycamore and chestnut are dominant. To reinforce this Garden of Eden experience, nuthatches and tree creepers are observed happily exploring the upper canopy for insects, while green and great spotted woodpeckers can be heard but not seen easily in the dense light green foliage. From a rustle ahead I am alerted to a deer bouncing of the path into the ferns, gazelle like, before rapidly accelerating out of view.

Despite this abundance of nature and wildlife I am saddened that in a copse of Scots pines — the habitat of the red squirrels — they are conspicuous by their absence. An observer's book of wild animals (1958) states that they are generally distributed in Great Britain and Ireland! Today we know they are only resident in pockets of northern Britain and Ireland or in Brownsea Island.

On my return to the Youth Hostel in Burley for a well-earned shower and refreshments at the adjacent and appropriately named White Buck Inn, a large tawny owl is flushed from its roost, in a hollow tree. Truly a day's New Forest experience.

7
The Othona Community — at Burton Bradstock, Dorset

Feeling like a break from the routine chores or even at the end of your tether? Then hang on, a visit to the Othona Community may be for you and can help to replenish you physically, mentally and spiritually.

The large stone house with attached chapel is set on the coast close to Burton Bradstock near Bridport, in grounds which are surrounded by National Trust and Nature Conservation areas. The house has been the home of the Othona Community for nearly twenty years but was the home of a group of women — the Christian Contemplative Charity — before that. Though a Christian Community with a warden and core members, today other faiths are also welcome, as are people seeking a deeper meaning to modern secular life and all enjoying the feeling of being in a community where God is love.

The prices are very reasonable, the furnishings are basic but adequate and the atmosphere is homely especially in the kitchen where you can help yourself to hot drinks at any time of the day or night. The food provided is wholesome, nourishing and sometimes includes vegetables from the kitchen-walled garden. The staff take the responsibility for cooking but require help in the preparation and with washing up where there are lots of volunteers.

Two short meditative services are held per day which are not obligatory but convenient since the chapel is attached to the main house via a corridor which reminds me of a monastery (not that I have ever been a monk!). It is best to have an open mind about other denominations since it does not seem to matter when chatting around a log fire, sharing a meal or communion. Running with someone on a beach you discover they are a minister trying to deal with inner city problems in London or homeless and enjoying a few days of relative comfort.

Since this is not a retreat but a community, children are welcome and my seven-year-old daughter enjoyed it from the start, as there were other children. An impromptu clay workshop to make pottery with your own turning wheel also impressed her. We did not attend any particular themed group during our weekend in October (though we have attended 'Let's make an Opera — Western worriers — Tribal trouble' before).

We are quite fond of birds, so one of the highlights was to go into the hills above Abbotsbury — home of a mute swannery — with Portland Bill peninsula as a backdrop on the coast, to see kestrels *Falco tinnunculus* and common buzzards *Buteo buteo*. En route back to Othona I stopped and through binoculars watched a pair of buzzards in flight coming together, joining talons and swinging around in celebration! This seemed to embody the wild spirit of Othona, being close to nature in a joyful embrace with others and our Creator.

8
'Oh, to soar like an Eagle' — sabbatical experience on the Isle of Arran, Scotland

Lord I come to you.

'And as I wait

I'll rise up like the eagle

And I will soar with You

Your Spirit leads me on

In the power of Your love'.

Have you ever noticed how often the eagle *Aquila chrysaetos* features in Christian song lyrics? There are also references to them in the Bible and a couple of lecterns in Churches in Lewes— at Southover plus St John Sub Castro (now Trinity Church). It begs the question: how many people have actually seen one in their lifetime? It is said the first time you see one it will be obvious. No ambiguity with other birds of prey. Its sheer majestic size and distinctive wing tips of individual feathers would set it apart.

However, I was confused. I had just started a whistle-stop tour to the glaciated valleys, in the northeast area, on the Isle of Arran. This must be the most accessible wilderness from Glasgow, Edinburgh and even London with overnight sleeper trains or cheaper dot com flights. Arran is described as 'Scotland in miniature' as it sits east of the Mull of Kintyre peninsula and in the Firth of Clyde. The locals stated that eagles are in the area and have been sighted. On the first afternoon, I set off up the 'Gleann Easan Biorach' in pursuit of its burn or river source — a small Loch called 'Na Davie'. I saw kestrels *Falco tinnunculus*, a sparrowhawk *Accipiter nisus*, even a large-shaped swallow called a merlin *Falco columbarius* travelling at lightning speed, but no eagles. I did wonder though, if the black silhouettes riding the thermals from a rocky outcrop of the local metamorphic schist over 300 metres high could be them? But from this distance without binoculars, they could be sparrows, though more likely common buzzards *Buteo buteo* known as the 'tourist's eagle' due to its more widespread abundance. Ironically many raptors have binocular vision, and they would have noticed my every movement even at this distance!

On return to sea level and the picturesque village of Lochranza, with its small castle sitting on a spit bank of shingle in the sheltered bay, I wondered if the red deer *Cervus elaphus,* that graze so nonchalantly were domesticated, such was their abundance? No, they are just taking advantage of the relative safety of the tourist season. The autumn hunting season will bring different tourists prepared to pay up to £1000 allegedly, to help stalk and cull deer. One can only hope this is a holistic and necessary operation using venison and not just a payment for a trophy of a stag's head and antlers to be displayed in some far (or near) flung place. Autumn also brings the rutting season, and I am reliably informed there is no better natural sight than a couple of stags strutting around their valley 'patch' proclaiming their territory (and the hinds that go with it) on a frosty, misty morning by bellowing with vapour steaming from their mouth. Quite a festive sight as long as you are not actively involved!

Glen Catacol beckons on a slightly better day with shafts of sunlight catching the green mosses, marsh plants, Killarney ferns *Trichomanes speciosum* and dominant purple heather *Erica carnea*. The route follows a beautiful river the 'Abhainn Mor' burn, flowing over slabs of granite and peat, producing the water which the distillers would have you believe helps to flavour Scots Whisky. After a few hours of walking, I am alerted to a scolding sound across the Glen. On looking up I see a couple of smaller birds mocking a Golden Eagle. It is unmistakeable — huge and supremely elegant — as it is preoccupied with wheeling, diving and ducking on wings bent to rid itself of this irritant. After a few flaps it soars and rises above its tormentors (we can learn from eagles) gliding along the mountain ridge covering in minutes the distance that it has taken us hours of plodding.

I am fortunate to share this moment with a young English family who had their heads down until the children latched onto what hopefully was a significant natural history moment for them. So not close enough to see the golden head but a positive sighting, nonetheless.

But those who hope in the Lord
will renew their strength.
They will soar on wings like eagles;
they will run and not grow weary,
they will walk and not be faint.
Isaiah 40: 31 (NIV, Bible).

9
The Golden Hare of Rathlin where legend meets science

You get a glimpse of what is in store for you as soon as the ferry from Ballycastle leaves and enters the choppy sea of Moyle across Rathlin sound to the Island. The six-mile journey to Church Bay is only twenty-five minutes on the big ferry, (forty-five minutes on the one-car ferry) but already stunning dapper black guillemots are glimpsed flying off at speed and was that a puffin that just went past?

There is a distinct Hebridean feel about this place with the seascape and rugged scenery, but on arrival at Northern Ireland's only inhabited island, it is confirmed by the habitat and people as uniquely akin to Ulster as you would expect. There are even two churches in the bay: St Thomas' a Church of Ireland or Anglican, Church of the Immaculate Conception, Roman Catholic, so Christians have choice. Rathlin sits three miles off the north Antrim coast at the closet point; to the east fourteen miles away is the Mull of Kintyre, whereas vistas to the west are of The Causeway Coast—a UNESCO World Heritage Site and eventually, Donegal. Islay and Jura lie to the north (the 'Paps of Jura' being visible on a good day!).

I arrived ready for a break after a strenuous time enduring the Ulster Way long distance walk — coastal and Moyle Way or Glens of Antrim section — and despite the solitary satisfaction of doing it, there was a dearth of biodiversity.

In Rathlin as well as helping me to recuperate, I knew I was guaranteed a species-rich wildlife fix and it delivered. There is a fresher (chillier) feel to the island but also a feeling of stepping back in time, due to the few roads and even fewer cars. The more traditional mixed farming and coastal habitat seem to favour rare species that are still in evidence, even if not common like the corncrake. Just walking around on the first day you can hear curlew, lapwing and skylark, while on the beaches the dominant calls are oystercatcher and redshank. You can also get really close to grey seals in Church Bay (close enough to observe them fighting and scratching) while in the adjacent Mill Bay there was a colony of thirty.

Rathlin is known for many things—allegedly Robbie the Bruce sought refuge in a cave and was inspired by a spider to have another go, early morse code signals were trialled to Ballycastle, and a fun, foot-tapping Maritime folk festival when Irish music is celebrated by bands with uilleann pipes, coming from all over Ireland, Scotland and Canada! However, it is especially known for the West Cliffs RSPB nature reserve at the West Point lighthouse. You can get a taxi from the ferry direct but my uncle and I decided to walk the two miles and enjoy the scenery. As an octogenarian he was wonderfully fit for his age but did need constant comfort breaks, bless him. He also taught me to collect the yellow gorse, furze or whin-bush blossom and rub the petals between my palms to emit an aroma of coconut spice. By doing this he demonstrated wonderfully well the passing on from one generation to another — an essential duty — of knowledge. Years later, I would share this knowledge with children and their parents of Indian heritage, when working in an urban park in west London, doing outdoor education activities.

Nothing can prepare you for the spectacular seabird fest as you turn a corner and see the giant stacks in the early summer, full of nesting, feeding chicks of kittiwakes, guillemots, razorbills and fulmars with puffins on the green grassy banks nearby. The cacophony of sound and intense guano smell will stay with you. Make sure you also try a boat trip and see the same birds as well as gannets fishing around other parts of the island from sea level.

When my dad and I first visited Rathlin, he was amused when we met an English gent resplendently dressed in a country cap, plus fours, brogues and binoculars. When asked what brought him to the island, he replied, 'the Irish hare!'. All hares belong to the *Lagomorpha* order in the mammal class and I was well aware that there was a difference between the brown hare, *Lepus europaeus* I see in the South Downs or Lowlands of England (range includes Europe and even parts of Asia), and the Irish hare I grew up with in Ireland *Lepus timidus hibernicus*. The Irish hare is different — a subspecies — to the Scottish mountain hare, *Lepus timidus* which turns white in winter and is found in the Highlands. Interestingly as far as the hare on the Island of Mull is concerned, DNA samples have proved that it has been introduced from the Irish mountain subspecies, and the brown hare, was also introduced to parts of Ireland, but now only exists in the northern parts of Ireland making the whole thing a bit complicated.

Intriguingly, on another occasion I arrived on the Island and the place was awash with press. The BBC's One Show had sent their wildlife enthusiast Mike Dilger to try to film Rathlin's golden hare. I had shared a lift with 'the crew' in a

Land Rover on my way to the Youth Hostel. Local artists have painted this beautiful mammal with golden fur and blue eyes against the backdrop of a full moon, giving it a legendary status! Great for Rathlin's tourist trade, but the legend is based on scientific fact, as a rare genetic mutation (caused by a recessive gene) in the Irish mountain hare subspecies has produced this beautiful quirky attraction. On reflection, that English gent knew more about natural history than we the locals gave him credit for.

On the last Sunday evening, I set off for a solitary walk, hoping to see the golden hare, but not too bothered as nature can disappoint if you set off looking for one thing but delights if you are open minded enough to enjoy whatever the journey turns up. The Roonavoolin walk, with the sun going down, was definitely the highlight of the trip. It is off the beaten track towards Rue Point, the most southerly point with 360 degrees, stunning subliminal seascapes including Fair Head on the Antrim coast to the south, the Mull of Kintyre to the east, two Outer Hebridean islands to the north and the Atlantic Ocean to the west. In reality the scenery just morphs together as one fest for the soul and is free of human place names. This RSPB nature reserve walk encourages you to walk safely along the cliffs with sheer drops (but you are safely behind a rope fence), and if lucky you will see Northern Ireland's only nesting choughs, *Pyrrhocorax pyrrhocorax,* riding the wind updraft, with their red beaks and legs. You would think these colourful charismatic corvids know they have a status as a conservation concern, the way they strut around on land too, looking for fly larvae called leatherjackets, while I enjoy true moments of surreal beauty.

Part 3 Awareness —

Encounters with the younger generation in mid-Sussex and west London as an outdoor educator, circa 2003–2018.

10
Old Chinese Proverb

I hear and I forget,
I see and I remember,
I do and I understand.

Anonymous.

11
A lesson in death!

Being a busy teacher in a secondary school in the heart of Sussex, I wondered if I was mad to be running an after-school club called 'RSPB Wildlife Explorers'. During the day of the club, I had registered that there was a dead female blackbird in the courtyard garden which was the venue for the "yellow perils" as they were colloquially known (due to bright fleeces and the free spirits it attracted). With three sets of windows around the garden in the middle of the school — two corridors and a library — the bird could have smashed into one. I made a mental note to 'get rid of it'. It would have distracted them from the planned activity to clear around the pond, as some sustainable garden furniture was due soon. However, I forgot, and should have notified the Site Manager. Too late, we had started, and eventually stumbled across the corpse as we opened up.

"There's a dead bird Sir!" said Peach with obvious emotional connection that I had underestimated.

"Ah yes," I answered, "I shall deal with this!"

I was looking for a nearby bush to gently push it under with the outside of my boot. As a humanities teacher which included RE, I felt I was suitably qualified to introduce death, which is a taboo subject in our society. They had obviously not had that lesson yet.

Marcel piped up "We should bury it properly!"

Susie helpfully replied, "I have an empty shoebox which I will get."

Things began spiralling out of control in a good way and I went with it as about five or six of us — after wrapping the shoebox with the specimen inside — walked towards the farm looking for a suitable burial ground. I think Olive asked if birds go to heaven and I was beginning to feel a bit out of my depth with my vague reply, when we arrived at the orchard, and the location was decided near a red Windsor apple tree by consensus. It was like a scene out of *Fantastic Mr Fox*: one tall, one small, one large but none of us mean. I had rapidly dug a very deep hole where the remains of the blackbird could rest for eternity.

The shoebox was carefully lowered, and soil covered it with the help of many little hands. The mood was now sombre and not a time for mirth nor, heaven forbid, a snigger from the 'grown-up'. I realised a formal response might be required as it went quiet, and I tried to keep up with the moment. Peach, the smallest girl, put her hands together in a prayerful pose and gave me a look as if to say *this is your bit*. I quickly followed suit and heard the words come from my own mouth: -

"Dear Father God, we thank you for the life of this blackbird, cut short so dramatically, it…"

Written May 2020 about club circa 2003.

12
Blue tit nest boxes — the good, the bad and the ugly

Fitting two nest boxes with cameras in a large secondary school was always going to be an education in working with children and animals. Little did I know then how much I was going to learn.

Location is everything. While one nest box in mature trees by the farm office seemed an ideal choice, perhaps in hindsight, the second in a wildlife garden courtyard adjacent to the library was not. In that location there was feeding competition from many species, so it was not ideal! The camera monitor in the library was rigged up to the camera in the nest box outside, on the other side of the wall by hard wire (today WiFi pairing gives more scope without the constraints of a wire). The librarian was interested, even enthusiastic, about the children having a creative viewing option especially if it was a wet break. I did say. "Remember you are in control, and you can always turn it off if it gets too distracting."

Both boxes got residents from the outset as they were set carefully at the right height and in the right direction (facing north-east), so it was game on. Blue tits, *Cyanistes caeruleus*, usually only have one clutch of eggs per year so, as the saying goes, they have all their eggs in one basket. They typically have about 8–10 eggs which are only 13mm long and white with very subtle red/ brown spotty speckles. We also observed that the female lays one per day, usually early in the morning, and she doesn't start incubating them until nearly all the eggs are laid, to synchronise hatching. The female blue tit has a brood patch of warm skin to help the process of incubation which lasts for about 14 days, and then they are fed as nestlings on average for 19 days in the security of the box, followed by support from both parents for a few weeks as fledglings outside the nest. Of the large brood only about three survive which is enough to propagate the next generation. The rest have accidents along the way and even sparrowhawks will pick a few up to feed their own chicks. Well, that is the theory, but as in all of the natural world, it is fun to discover that nature hasn't always read the book.

Students would gather around the monitor, observing the nest making with much excitement, and I would have a group of 'Wildlife Explorers' who would record special events in a nature diary. I was one of the first into that part of the school in the morning, so I would routinely turn on the monitor and spend a few moments in awe at the intimate sights inside the nest box. The Headteacher and other colleagues were kept in touch as one egg after another was laid. I even reported in the school magazine under the pseudonym of 'Cyril the Squirrel' so parents could follow the first egg hatching.

After a few days of the chicks feeding on caterpillars from a nearby oak, all was well, until a wet Monday. Imagine my horror when, as I was teaching in a room up the corridor from the library, in the middle of a lesson the librarian burst in, distraught, and said "Mr Melville! A large bird has just entered the nest box and is thrashing it and the blue tit!"

I left the teaching assistant in charge and accompanied the

librarian back to the library. I also witnessed a larger brown bird being aggressive as the female blue tit cowered in the corner with wings displayed defensively, trying desperately to defend her brood. What could I do in the puzzlement but just stay calm and turn off the monitor? As a rule, I do not interfere with nature in all its tooth and claw (a wider argument that will not be dealt with here). As a school, many were emotionally involved anthropomorphically in this blue tit's life cycle — unbeknown to it — as I returned to class somewhat crestfallen and baffled, not in any mood to expand. My thoughts were whirling, since we had a strong nest box with a steel plate around the entrance to provide access for blue tits/great tits only (28mm diameter).[1] This deters great spotted woodpeckers and squirrels from widening the hole and predating the eggs/chicks. However, I finished the lesson, set homework and saw my Tutor Group off.

After school was not a Wildlife Club night so I could return to the library and had the grim job of turning on the monitor to witness the aftermath of the scene of carnage! To make matters worse the male parent blue tit had just turned up with a juicy caterpillar but was confused at the entrance at the lack of interest. What could have squeezed through the entrance? It had all happened so fast but at least the parent blue tit seemed to have escaped. In the courtyard we had a feeding station which had many species using it — three species of tits, chaffinches and house sparrows, to name a few. In fact, the house sparrows also nested in another part of the school in a social nest box of three together. All nests were occupied and even observed by carefully lifting the top hinged flap from a

---

[1] The diameter of nest box plates for blue tits is 25mm.

safe but usually inaccessible balcony, in what was a fairly chaotic nest style compared to the blue and great tits. I had to conclude that the sparrow must have been the culprit due to the competition for food and nest space, though on the monitor it did seem more starling size, such was the challenge in monitor scale perspective. My suspicions were confirmed when I later passed the courtyard en route for home that wet cool evening for May, as there on top of the nest box could clearly be seen a male 'cock' house sparrow. His whole display said "this is my patch" as he chirped and bounced with his wings at a jaunty angle.

Despite the emotional rollercoaster of this incident, we learnt a lot about lowering our expectations or not counting our chicks before they are hatched (sorry), as well as the practical challenges of getting the diameter size of the steel plate correct for the target species, in this case a blue (not great) tit. Also, being philosophical: nests and eggs do not have a 100% success rates with inexperienced parents, nature predations and though nest box number two on the farm had regular broods of blue tits nearly all fledging! There was a deep connection and richness for the 'Wildlife Club' members observing more easily the courtyard nest box. Many others observed the first eggs laid and hatched nestlings appearing, all recorded on video. The next example gives a more positive outcome.

While watching the monitor with Libby one morning we were intrigued to see that after feeding and removing the poo pack, the parent blue tit accidently flicked a nestling who got entangled with her feet as she exited, from the comfort of the snug nest to the outer reaches of the nest box!

I said, "Quick Libby turn on the video recorder!" and the following outcome I shared with 300 or 400 children — lower school or Key Stage 3 — in assembly the following week. The blue tit nestlings were very dependent on their parents, so at about six days old these chaps didn't have their eyes open yet or much down to keep them warm. We wondered if the chick would survive being away from its siblings in the warm nest, or perish? To the music of M People's 'You got to search for the hero inside yourself', the video was simultaneously shown on the big screen. There was much interest and encouragement as the chick slowly crawled up and over the nest edge before falling back in the nest instinctively, to the loud cheering and clapping of the whole hall. It is a moment I will never forget.

Written June 2020 about nest boxes circa 2002–2006.

13
The dog incident

"Freeze! Freeze!" All the children stood like statues until I said "Relax!". As drills go, this was one of the best ways to prepare them, in the relative safety of the visitor's centre forecourt, to go out into the wilds of the Country Park in west London, where they could meet random members of the public and their dogs. Importantly it also satisfied the risk assessment for the local school and the Christian Conservation Charity I had been working for, for over eight years.

For an outdoor educator, an urban park like this was priceless and a fantastic place for British-born, first-generation children from the Indian community (the Punjab region), to engage with nature's classroom. The old English water meadow had habitats and species of grasslands, woodland and wetlands nearby to enjoy, and these children loved learning outside, even if tentative to start with. The irony was that, despite being taught by parents to swat insects, especially bees, and that dogs were probably fierce as they had only met guard dogs, the Sikh religion and agrarian community of their heritage were probably farmers who owned/worked the land. Somehow on arrival in the UK they had skipped this connection. So, we had to break down barriers even with some of the staff, but it didn't take long with these outstanding schools. I mean their Holy

Scriptures from the Gurus, including Nanak, laid down in the Guru Granth Sahib respect for ecology. Caring for creation unites rather than divides faiths.

So, the plan was that, if a dog was running ahead of its owner, stand still with hands by your side and let the lead adult deal with it. At least that was the theory. The 'Freeze! Freeze!' was only to be used in an emergency to stop the children. While I or the lead teacher was discussing with the owner and getting the dog on a lead, another member of staff would calmly round up the children and lead them back to school. Up until today, I had never had to use it, but it felt secure having it in place ready, especially as this school was relatively new to the activities. The six-year-olds had to be treated with kid gloves.

The day could not have been better, with sunshine and blue skies, the only clouds being those wispy mares' tails. Today we would be pond dipping or rather 'active stream' dipping for invertebrates. Now sometimes in the spring/summer weather the water level can be low, making it difficult for catching anything in the net, as the stream churns up mud and, I am sure, stressing the creatures too. But today we were blessed with a good quantity of water, due to the unusual high rainfall at this time of the year. We always had a carousel of stimulating activities, so half the class was dipping for dragonfly and damselfly nymphs, caddisfly larva, minnows, snails (both pond and ramshorn), scorpion and other water beetles plus, if very lucky, leeches. The other half were on another small bridge further downstream, doing a mixture of recording their survey results, sketching and looking through an underwater endoscope to see the above creatures in their watery home instead of a white tray. All was well with the world.

Suddenly I saw a large greyhound bounding up to us and for the first time, I had to say, "Freeze! Freeze!", which the children duly did! I could see that the dog, without any owner in sight, was not fierce but excited, playful even from its wide eyes and the lolling tongue, it thought it was game on. Almost in slow motion I saw it stopping at one young girl who did her best to remain stationary as the greyhound squared up to her eyeball to eyeball. At this point, unsurprisingly, she decided to bolt for it, and this caused a chain reaction as other children followed suit! Nets, trays of water with minibeasts went flying as the greyhound ran amok and interpreted this as a game of chase. I knew that this was the end of the lesson but noticed in the ensuing pandemonium, a bit late for his cue, an unfit and heavily puffing owner come running down the path stage left. I and the other staff were so surprised at how quickly the quiet order had been turned to chaos by the dog, that we didn't say a thing as the owner brought the hyper greyhound under control, with the use of a lead. He mumbled something under his breath, maybe sorry, as he quickly headed on his way.

With the children so visibly shaken, we rapidly gathered our equipment and finished. Two more classes in the afternoon were cancelled by the school as the school had to deal with the fallout from the children's exaggerated stories. You can just imagine in the playground — Anisha had to run for her life when the dog tried to attack her, etc, etc. I thought it was harsh decision but realised the school had to phone the individual parents to give them the true version of the story, quite a PR exercise with so much rumour spreading like wildfire. I also felt a bit crestfallen that as it was practically the first time this school had participated, it was now probably their last as well, and I was more than a bit angry at the owner to whom I should have at least spoken. Philosophically, I understood that there are many uses for urban country parks; environmental education is only one of them, and no matter how much you plan or assess risk, you can never eliminate it totally in this park, open to the public.

I didn't need to worry, as in a few weeks I had a phone call from the Science Coordinator, saying they were ready to go again, and of course they understood the value of the activities, in enriching the curriculum learning for children despite the risks; besides, the school understood that dogs with walkers are not dangerous. I dusted down the plan and looked at the Health and Safety starter — Freeze! Freeze! yes, definitely be keeping that in!

14
Can I have my teddy back please? The dilemmas of using quiet park spaces

The adaptation of Michel Rosen's poem 'We're going on a Bear Hunt' from successful book to the big screen was an expected progression for all who know and love it. However, I thought, as a way of introducing children as young as four years old to the natural world, it could be improvised in an urban country park setting, as they were introduced in a tactile way to different habitats, stimulating all the senses. I called it outward bound for 'Littlies' and it was manna from heaven for an outdoor educator. I was proud when I arrived as a newbie that it was already popular for the children to walk around chanting the chorus before being introduced to the grass, water, mud and forest, but I gave it my own twist going deeper into the wild parts.

Most children enjoyed the journey through the grasslands, woodlands and wetlands 'en route' to searching for the bear — very large teddy — whom they meet at the end. There were exceptions, as this was for most the first time in such a natural place, and it was exciting but overwhelming. One child who had a couple of adults each side of her screamed the whole way, probably sparked off when she touched a stinging nettle. Interestingly, at the end she wanted to do it all again!

The season of the year was important, as it was dramatic in winter with frost and snow on the ground but the small river they crossed was nearly over the top of wellies and the mud was so thick that boots would be sucked in. The children followed each other in a slow, snakelike procession, and it reminded me of the winter scene from C S Lewis' *The Lion, the Witch and the Wardrobe*.

However, due to the cold hands of all, plus the necessary drying out of much clothing on return to school (mainly gloves) the tamer summer term was generally favoured by the parents of such young precious children.

It was not always appreciated that there was a large amount of preparation for the bear route around the urban park which usually took place the day before by two adults using a scythe, loppers and litter pickers to make it accessible, especially if it was the first bear hunt event of the year. If you clear too many obstacles, it makes it sterile, so there was a tension between clearing and leaving some thistles, briars and nettles. The dilemma was that by doing it the evening before, as well as seeing birds and animals — ring-necked parakeets, two species of woodpecker, little owls, kestrels, sparrowhawks and the odd fox — the quieter woody places also attracted 'human wildlife'. The local council also had trouble here allegedly with flash mob raves too. I used to wonder what the people were like who frequented these places by the litter they left behind — Haribos and condoms? I was about to find out.

On the day of 'The Bear Hunt' it was a scorcher. I was asked by the school leader if it should still go ahead, since parents were concerned. Of course, I said, as long as the nursery children were well covered, had sun block and plenty of drinks. Heathrow Airport later reported it as a record-breaking 34 degrees centigrade! Good weather also draws in other 'celebrities' as co-users of the park and I knew it was going to be an interesting day, since during the morning scope, I came across a homeless person on the route in the vicinity of the 'Bear Cave'. I spoke calmly to him, explaining that in an hour we hoped to bring about sixty people around, including small children. It is an area of challenge, in my experience, when you meet people who overnight in these public places, possibly due to a mixture of family rejection, addiction, physical and mental health issues beyond my and my organisation's specialism. We can, though, be compassionate and treat them with respect; this I did and offered him bottled water as he reluctantly headed for the park bench. I knew that I would have to inform the lead teacher that we could come across people like this person en route as it was such a good weather day. I also carried a smaller teddy bear in my rucksack in the event that we couldn't use the final part of the route: the Bear Cave.

The lead teacher was robust and agreed with my risk assessment that it was not a major hazard. Off we went, the children chanting the first lines of the chorus 'We're going on a Bear Hunt...' I also noticed that a few parents had buggies and clutched the younger siblings of those taking part, but we even had an alternative route for them to enjoy, where they could take photos without going through the stream or mud. It was going well, apart from one parent helper who had slipped in the mud! Many of the adults did not have wellies like the children and tried to jump by lunging at the other bank without any help from the male helper. This woman had landed in the middle of my improvised mud bed with litres of water poured over the dry stream to create a quagmire!

We had just finished the verse and stumbled through the forest or small wood copse (one of my favourites) and paused to use our imagination as to how to do the next verse of a snowstorm in July! A long grassy area was good to run and spin around in, to improvise a snowstorm, going "Woo hoo!", and the rumble of the traffic on the adjacent parkway provided the sound of the wind. We were in full flight, spinning and wooing when I noticed that unusually we had an audience. Sitting near the end of the path by an old oak tree was a small bohemian group of people wearing bandana head scarfs and beads and a few with leather hats having drinks and watching in silence. They must have wondered what we were doing!

When we got to the end, I got everyone quiet and calm by saying "Listen, listen, did you hear that?"

As usual, nearly all the children heard a bear snoring as we approached the Bear Cave, with camouflage netting enclosing a huge teddy for the last verse. As we tiptoed towards it with a mixture of excitement, trepidation and whispers, I heard voices of people coming from the Bear Cave! Our imaginary chamber also doubled this day as a haven social area for local drinkers. Plan B with the rucksack-sized teddy was sprung into action and while a bit of an anti-climax, enabled us to finish securely without any interruptions from the public.

On completion, I was a bit annoyed, but most parents were unaware of any changes. However, I did want our 'teddy' back. So, after seeing the children go off in the right direction I went back to the cave for my resources and found a large fellow enjoying an amber liquid sitting on teddy. I asked if I could please have it back and mumbled something about school resources.

He sat up and said very apologetically, "Sorry mate, I thought someone had just abandoned it here."

I can't imagine what the 'revellers' thought as I stomped off with a giant teddy underneath my arm. I was thinking that, despite sharing such a wonderful urban park, we thankfully have never had any major problems with the eclectic public and their very diverse reasons for using it.

Post Script.
This is not an isolated case as a colleague of mine had a similar experience. She was working as a beekeeper in a community garden doing similar activities — introducing children to nature — using an observation hide at a bee apiary in an urban area. She had to regularly check the beekeeper's shed before the children's groups arrived as it was occasionally used by homeless people whom she treated with respect and compassion by providing contact details for the local church's night shelter. She had to be aware of the potential for distraction. If the shed was not checked, someone could appear from the shed during the middle of the lifecycle of the honeybee. On return to class there could have been much discussion on homelessness in our society as well as of biology in the curiculum!

Part 4 Acceptance —

Close encounters when settled in the South Downs, Sussex circa 2000s 2010s, with flying visits to the Emerald Isle and East Africa.

15
FOX

I met him in the woodland
above a rocky shore
basking in the sunshine
head resting on his paw

ears pricked up
he raised his head
sniffed the air
and then he saw-

our gazes met
eyes locked in stares
surprise, astonishment and fear
I froze, he froze,
then tossed his head
sprang up and bounded off,
leaping over fern and stone
he paused, looked back at me
then with a swish
of bushy tail
my tawny friend
was gone
leaving me only a glimpse

of the white tip of his tail

and a sense of gratitude
that I had been blessed
by this encounter
with a magnificent wild creature.

By Shirley Darlington November 23rd, 2017, Printed by kind
permission from the author.

16
To sound like a demented mouse?

I was walking from work one glorious summer evening, along the seafront between Newhaven and Seaford—a nature reserve called Tide Mills. Skylarks were singing on the Downs side, when I was stopped in my tracks, seeing a huge bird gliding over this terrain. From a distance, I could see it came to rest on a post, half a mile further on! I quickly deduced that if I discreetly passed it by, I could quietly run along the lower end of a sand dune type embankment, before popping up adjacent to it. So, I dropped the briefcase (there were few people around in this land/sea margin), bent over nearly double and 'voila' the bird of prey! I was however initially disappointed, as it was an owl, when I was expecting a hen harrier or something of that ilk, but it was an owl I had not seen before. On researching at my 'digs' I discovered it was a short-eared owl, *Asio flammeus,* which had a metre wingspan! I was quite pleased with my field study skills though, which were being rehoned after being dormant for many years while being immersed in young family life. I was also in a reflective mood, between moving counties — Kent to Sussex. This other journey I was reluctantly contemplating was as an 'absent father', the legal term for the parent who lives away, which I hated, even though it was physically right. So, I was grateful for nature's solace.

Eventually, I bought a small farm labourer's end of terrace house, in a hamlet, in the Ouse Valley just south of the county town of Lewes. I learnt more about these owls 'overwintering' (they nest in moorlands further north in the UK), and their distant relatives the barn owls — *Tyto alba* — on my patch of the valley. They would only appear in the Ouse Valley when one of their main food sources — the field, or short-tailed vole — was not abundant in other valleys. Rising early at the weekend, on a very wintery morning, was the best way to see them. If you walked to the scruffy grass edges near the river, stood as stationary as a fence pole, or even leant against one to blend in, with binoculars at the ready, you could be rewarded with this owl focussing on the grass as it nearly stalled in flight, like a giant moth. Eventually big yellow eyes would stare up at you, rapidly 'turning on a sixpence', it continues quartering vole territory, with its beautiful brown striated feathering beating into the distance.

I shared many a wildlife encounter like this one, with a church warden friend, who though a builder/roofer by trade, was a very knowledgeable mature countryman.

One day when discussing owls, he enlightened, "If you hold your fist to your mouth and make a kissing sound, like a demented mouse, the owl will fly towards you."

Later, I was having a solitary walk, in particularly high spirits having had something to celebrate but there was not a lot to see. I had only gone about three quarters of a mile when, wow! A short-eared owl silently appeared close by! I had not seen one so far from the river before. I remembered the

74

conversation with the warden and immediately started kissing the back of my hand, straight away the owl reacted by kinking its flight towards me! It actually flew right over, looking down, before turning and coming back again. On return it even made a mock lunge at me, that was when I thought how wise is this? By pretending to have a mouse as bait, to a creature that had all that arsenal at its disposal, in the form of a pair of talons, it was not without risk. Instinctively I stopped and the owl, by this time quite confused, came to rest across a small dyke in a field about ten metres away. Still looking at me, it ruffled its feathers doing some information gathering, before departing on its quest for some real prey.

Occasionally I find a pellet on a post or a stile. A pellet is just the regurgitated dry remains that the owl or other bird of prey could not digest: bits of feathers, small bones, etc. I find them fascinating as they are a little capsule of evidence into what the creature has been eating, but I am aware not everyone is enthusiastic about them. They don't smell and children love to take them apart, with tweezers in a tray with some hot water. If you find any miniscule bones or even a small skull, you can have great fun identifying which vole, mouse or small bird it has had for supper.

There is a sequel to the above close encounter with a short-eared owl. I have lived in the same house for over twenty years and 'dandered' around my patch while volunteering for the BTO's survey — Bird Atlas 2007–2011 — covering an area of sixteen square kilometres. I was aware that I veered off the beaten track or public rights of way. I have met a few tenant farmers and even hunters, and believe good communication and honesty are best. A symbiotic relationship can be formed, where I have reported any beasts in trouble, like cattle stuck in the dyke, and they put up with my trespassing. However, there are limits: the hunters have been generous in their offerings to me — a semi-vegetarian — by saying, "help yourself to a brace of wood pigeon for supper, stacked at the end of the lane." We share an interest in the same species; however, I would not go as far as telling them where I had seen the last snipe! This particular winter, there were reports that about six short-eared owls were patrolling regularly in the valley. They had been seen nearly every evening in the area of the next village, so I thought I would have an extra walk on 'my patch'. There were more owls than I had ever seen before. Though the owls were not close, I started the hand-kissing gestures, which if anything had the opposite effect! I was in the middle of disturbing them, when something made me turn my binoculars towards the village. My solitude evaporated as I saw an array of telescopes all trained in my direction. The spotter had become the spotted.

17
Stoats — Mutual Curiosity

I don't recall ever seeing a stoat, *Mustela erminea hibernicus* in Northern Ireland, up until the time I left in my mid-twenties. In Ireland the common name for the stoat is a weasel and there are no weasels (in the Scots dialect, which parts of Ulster share, it is known as Whutret or Whitrat from white rat). The Irish stoat does not turn white (or partially white) in winter, a transformation known as ermine. On the stoat's body, the dividing line between the dark brown upper fur and the white lower fur is straight in England and irregular in Ireland! Meanwhile, the difference between a stoat *Mustela erminea* and a weasel *Mustela nivalis* in England, are that stoats are longer at 30–40cm, compared with weasels at 20–27cm. Stoats also have a longer tail—about half its body length, with a bushy black tip. In addition, the stoat has a bounding 'gait' with an arched back, whereas the movement of the weasel is quicker and flatter to the ground.

Living deep in the South Downs National Park, walking and driving around in my trusted Citroen 2CV, I was aware of the presence of mustelids, on numerous occasions. My daughter and I glimpsed them en route back from Breaky Bottom Vineyard and, on frosty mornings in the Ouse Valley, a little head would pop out a few times as you walked along. After a particularly good BBQ, when folks had gone, and before the final clear up, it was not unusual for a hedgehog or rodent to appear, such were the appetising smells wafting around the flint-walled garden. This evening, something was snaking up through the wild strawberry corridor at the base of the wall at speed. Could it really have been a stoat or weasel in the twilight darkness? With all these 'partial' sightings it is very hard to positively identify the species. My farmer neighbour said anecdotally that in these parts it would only be a stoat and there is usually 'some' truth in local knowledge.

I have a regular patch that I walk and enjoy observing the seasons, especially through one particularly woody, watery copse intersection between fields that I was later to name 'stoat alley'. Most days there is no sign of them, but when they do arrive, it's almost likely that they stay a few days in a row, and it is worth making an extra trip. First, adult stoats could be seen carrying something in their mouths (baby stoats — kits, or baby rabbits — kittens): it is hard to say as they both look lifeless. Bloodcurdling screams could be heard when a hunt is going on. Sometimes a rabbit that is being hunted will stop on a path quite near you, as if trying to use you as a decoy, while the stoat is in pursuit though quite far behind. An abandoned dead rabbit is also worth watching from a distance, as the stoat, if it has been disturbed, will definitely come back for it. But my best encounter happened on a random evening which I now recall as follows here: -

"Just had an incredible close encounter with a stoat down a country lane from my place where I have seen many stoats before, but not for a couple of years. I was alerted, when two partridge were flushed out but more relevantly, a robin, wren and whitethroat were all scolding something below. Minutes later, an adult stoat was frolicking around in some scrubby ground among the ragwort about five metres from me. Rolling, tumbling and even jumping up and kicking his legs in the air. I didn't need my binoculars but got a close-up of this feisty little predator. He didn't appear to see me as I froze to the spot like one of his rabbit prey, hypnotised by its antics. Then he darted across the track and came bounding up the edge of the ferns, almost passing and stopped 1/2 a metre from me, suddenly intrigued! When he looked like coming towards me,

I shuffled my feet in my bare foot sandals as I felt he might take a liking to my toes! He bolted into the cover but came out again at least twice to check me out, such was his curiosity. The secret of my close encounters like this is stillness and silence (easy when you are on your own). Sadly, if I was talking to another, I don't think we would have seen the stoat at all. They just can't understand a silent human without motion, and I have got as close to a brown hare, roe deer, grey squirrel and red fox, using the same tactic, except with the hare it smelled me first (yes, I know) rather than me deliberately spooking it."

This story was first posted on Facebook — 27th June 2015
16:52

18
Too close for comfort

As a follow-up to the last story — Stoats mutual curiosity — I will share more on the close encounters with the red fox, *Vulpes vulpes* and the roe deer, *Capreolus capreolus*. Both have excellent traits at detecting us humans but can be outsmarted.

Very often foxes hear or smell you before you see them, due to your careless noise, like the clanging when climbing over a gate. If you are oblivious to the wind direction and they are downwind from you, it is not in your favour. For example, when the prevailing wind is behind you and you reek of the latest African spice deodorant, coconut shampoo and Spanish fig and nutmeg aftershave (and that's just the men). To be incognito, it is best to have natural smells and colours. From a distance, if the fox has not seen you, enjoy the moment with binoculars, but be aware that when it scans its horizon periodically it will not always react if it sees you. It will just calmly get on with things before bolting when it next gets into cover. Foxes are canny creatures, as any hunter will tell tales of the one that got away. They deserve our respect, though, for their survival, despite the odds in both the rural and urban environments.

Imagine my surprise one day when I had just arrived at a favourite vantage point by a gate post, to notice an adult dog fox ambling along fifty metres away, between the thistles on the field margin, coming in my direction. It had a beautiful healthy looking bright red/brown coat and a long bushy tail. I stood my ground, but quickly realised it was heading right towards me, probably to get through the bars in the gate where I was standing. My heart started to beat faster, so at about two metres away I intuitively gave up my cover and said "hello". He stopped dead in his tracks, and we just stared at each other momentarily. I had never noticed the bright orange eyes with flecks of black before, like staring into the wild. In the next flash he bolted full pelt for the middle of the field. He stopped, looked round as if to say, "What just happened there? How could I have been so off guard?" He then resumed his running, not quite so frantic, but still intentionally putting many metres between us, wow!

More amusing was an experience I had on the long-distance footpaths of the North Downs Way from Farnham in Surrey to Dover in Kent. A lovely undulating way, with much of it tree lined, that in places follows the Pilgrims Way to Canterbury. If you're lucky in spring, you can see the young of many creatures, including birds, rabbits and foxes such is the fecundity of the area. On this day, a dog owner had lost control of their Alsatian. The dog had seen me from a distance of a field and a half, so I started running, perhaps maybe not the best thing to do. On turning a corner, I saw a fox rooting in the soil in the middle of a small field. Surprisingly, it didn't see or hear me, and I had little time to observe it as I ran past, holding my rucksack tightly. I knew it would provide the perfect decoy for intercepting the Alsatian as I crossed over a stile and entered the woods. Sure enough, I could hear loud barking behind, as I pressed onwards now without having to run.

I got close to a deer in the Surrey Hills — an area of outstanding natural beauty — near Ranmore Common in the Tanners Hatch, Youth Hostel and Polesdon Lacey, National Trust area. If anything, prey species like deer and hares are even trickier to get close to, due to their highly developed alertness. However, the same skills apply, and if we observe predator creatures that prey on them, like the African big cats, for example, that we see on the TV — masters of sleuth — it is a mixture of stealth and swiftness. Conversely, stepping on a twig will give the game away. It was in the autumn season and a young roe deer buck was feeding solitarily among the ferns. I latched on to it with 100% concentration, forgetting everything else. I stood motionless every time it raised its head and likewise, when it was distracted by grazing, I advanced a few metres at a time, being careful where I put my feet. I was pleasantly surprised to be within a metre of it after a longer than usual head-down graze. I could have reached out and touched it, but at this moment I decided not to, respecting that this was a wild animal, and I instinctively thought it was a line I should not cross. It should be on their terms, plus there was a safety risk for both as it had short stumpy antlers and hard hooves. Its reaction when it realised how close I was, confirmed my decision as the correct one, as it 'detonated' into active flight but thankfully not fight mode.

19
'There's a bat in the house!'

Though originally from the province, I had not been to a barbeque in County Antrim for many years, despite frequent visits. Living in the southeast of England, in the last few summers there had been lots of opportunities to have BBQs in July and August as the weather has become predictably hot and humid. Five weeks prior to my Northern Irish holiday we had hosepipe bans and droughts; my rainwater harvesting butts were empty again. My farmer neighbour stretched one evening with a full stomach and said, "Why are you going over there anyway, it might rain?"

The country house location near Crumlin could not have been a better setting, with views over 'The Largy' —Lough Neagh basin farmland. A barbeque had been arranged by one married partner for the other, as a surprise fiftieth birthday party. Both were dear friends, spanning thirty years of my visits to old home. The venue had a walled garden patio and arch, all made from local recycled stone, with enhancements of outdoor heater and parasols, for sun or rain I wondered? It was always going to be different, I had just enjoyed a lovely holiday in the Hebrides and Ulster, but I had not worn sockless sandals since leaving Sussex. There were, however, rain clouds looming ominously.

Guests arrived suitably clad for the cooler clime, and the

main course was enjoyed amongst much spitting of meat being cooked. Soon the spitting from the hood of the heater indicated that, as the rain had started, it was time to clutch a plate and go inside. This did not dampen the spirits though, and the 'craic' continued in the dining room, where an array of sumptuous desserts had appeared, mysteriously. My favourite was a marshmallow type of mousse laced with sherry and my teenage daughter was enjoying a rich chocolate pudding, which she said was helping with some bad news.

Suddenly my daughter exclaimed, "What is that inside the lampshade?" A dark shape could be seen trying to climb the light bulb but slipping down like some sort of flickering light gadget, only it was off.

"It's a bat!" wailed the hostess, who usually appreciates wildlife. "I thought there was a bat in here," she exclaimed, referring to a surreal moment she must have had earlier. Now the reaction to a bat in the house is pretty mixed, ranging from horror to almost loving care, depending on your enthusiasm for natural history. Most were moved at the sight of a pipistrelle, in such an inappropriate place. The most curious are those at primary school, who come running to see and want to take it home. With great care, as there is not much room between a bulb and its glass shade, the bat was taken outside between two serviettes and placed gingerly on the wall in the rain. It licked itself a few times and then crawled over the edge to find shelter, chill and hang out, just like us really!

On my return to Sussex, I was glad to notice that at dusk, pipistrelles come out. They enjoy eating the insects in my organic wildlife garden, including moths hovering around the buddleia. This reminds me of a special moment, during an Irish barbeque indoors.

Written for BBC Radio Ulster and the Belfast Telegraph, 'My Story' was a BBC Northern Ireland series. The Senior Producer enjoyed reading this, but it was not published due to the series ending.
— August 2006.

Postscript: There is an adjunct to this story. Years later, when recalling it with the host and hostess, they said it was not the first or last bat they had seen in the house. When this happened one evening, Grandad, who lived just down the road, was called. A known countryman, he deftly caught the bat in his soft cap before releasing it unharmed. Now there is a skill to teach the next generation.

20
What a difference a day makes. Forest adventure in West Rwanda, East Africa

Seeing a close-up of an adult male olive baboon *Papio anubis*, was the icing on the cake of a great morning wildlife watching, in the Kingdom of Cyamudongo Forest Park, western Rwanda. Our guide spoke quietly, after listening intently, reading the baboon's behaviour. This special monkey was now perched on a tree branch, a few metres above the path the guide was encouraging us to use! It had been barking quite aggressively, since we stumbled upon it running at speed towards us, on the same thoroughfare, before immediately diving into the thick vegetation and reappearing at its current vantage point. The mid-morning sun was coming up fast, as we wearily trudged back to our base, after our four a.m. start. Hopefully this beautiful creature was just putting on a show, as it yawned, displaying its huge incisors. It was the same feeling of bluff you experience when faced with an unknown but fearful dog. They have the capability of attacking and inflicting damage, but would they? In the melee, I had got separated from Annette, my wife, who was accompanying me on this trip for her first time. Our group walked in respectful single file, towards the Land Rovers. I was at the end with an amateur photographer, as we held our breath, on passing underneath our third primate of the tour. When we had gained a few metres, the photographer turned and captured a few more images. Thankfully, the sound of the lens shutter did not set the baboon off; instead, he just looked nervously down at us. The thought did cross my mind, if he had decided to come down, he could make the few metres between us very rapidly. What could we have done with our sticks? It was quite a dramatic finish to a wonderful morning and, as if to reinforce the tension of it all, my wife said to me quietly, "Where were you when I needed you most?" to which I replied, "I was bringing up the rear," in a mock protective way for the group. I realised I was bluffing as much as the baboon.

'*Muraho*' and *'Amahoro'* mean hello and peace; what a wonderful blessing to visit the 'Land of a thousand hills' Rwanda, in East Africa, many times over the last decade. My local church — Trinity Lewes — had a big team, carrying out worthy practical projects in rainwater harvesting, healthcare, business micro-finance, Mothers' Union handicrafts, English and eco-tourism teaching, to name but a few. Our integration with the development in this country had a mutual benefit as we always came back enriched. I was motivated by reaching out to their plight, in response to the genocide that took place in 1994. However, the groundwork had been done by a couple, who had been missionaries in the region — both fluent in Kinyarwanda — and more recently by a stalwart, who had been based in-country for over three years. In this natural history encounter though, I am going to focus on our downtime activities, which I am proud to say I encouraged from the start. Visits now to Rwanda's wonderful wild places have become a routine, optional extra part of the itinerary as recreation for groups that have followed. You may already have heard of Rwanda's iconic flagship species, the mountain gorilla *Gorilla gorilla beringei*, surely one of the great conservation stories of our generation. Dian Fossey is known for bringing to the world's attention their plight and helping set up protection plus sustainable eco-tourism for the world to see them in the Volcanoes National Park or 'Virunga'. For similar 'mega bucks', they can also be viewed by tours set up in Uganda, from Bwindi, the impenetrable forest and the Democratic Republic of Congo, who share access to the same dormant volcanoes mountainous habitat. Savannah experiences can

89

also be enjoyed in the east of Rwanda at Akagera National Park, bordering Tanzania, where a big five can be viewed: elephant, buffalo, hippopotamus, crocodile, antelopes, and if lucky, leopard. For marshland birds and otters, the beautiful Rugezi Wetlands — a RAMSAR International site — at Musenda, Gicumbi District, near Byumba, is a convenient mid-stop from Kigali to the Virunga.

Travelling southwest from Kigali to Cyangugu (*the land beyond the forest*, such a lovely African expression), on the border of the DRC, you travel through a National Forest Park called Nyungwe (pronounced N-yoong-gway).[2] I was immediately impressed by the richness of this forest, with L'Hoests mountain monkeys *Allochrocebus lhoesti* (conservation status vulnerable, IUCN) an endemic in this area, on the roadside as we passed by. Nyungwe is a biological hotspot and the largest montane forest in Central Africa — one thousand square kilometres of well-managed habitat, which includes Burundi's Kibira National Park to the south, to which it is contiguous. The forest rises from Lake Kivu and the DRC in the west, from 1600 to 2950m (5200–9680 feet), the watershed between the Congo and Nile (which is one of the sources of this great river). The region is special for biodiversity, due to the geography of sharing part of the Albertine Rift Valley and the Ruwenzori Mountain range. It is primate heaven: fourteen species, including the only ape—the

---

[2] Cyangugu is the old name of one of the 12 former Provinces in Rwanda but is now a city at the southern end of Lake Kivu in Rusizi District. Cyangugu is also the capital of Rusizi District and in the newly formed Western Province (one of 5 Provinces along with Northern, Southern, Eastern and Kigali) set up in 1996, post genocide. The Anglican church has retained the name Cyangugu Diocese.

eastern chimpanzee *Pan troglodytes schweinfurthii* (Conservation status endangered, IUCN). On many of the walks, it is a challenge to see mammals or the 280 bird species clearly, such is the opulence of the trees. From previous visits, our guide had drawn our attention to the sounds of the great blue turaco and a golden cat. I also knew it was wise to leave the forest before dusk, since side-striped jackals would start to roam from their caves, which were also home to black cobras living at the entrance! Other aspirations would be to see the African crowned eagle, with its two-metre wingspan, which is a specialist in catching monkeys in the canopy as prey. The biggest troupe of black and white Angola colobus monkeys *Colobus angolensis ruwenzori*, about 400, can be found in the thick of the forest—that is ten times bigger than you will find in any other part of Africa. However, there is an excitement or a spirit of the wild, knowing that rare predators like leopards could be passing through or even watching you on your journey (as they will definitely see you first). The only other time I have ever experienced this in Europe was on a visit to A Rocha in the south of France. When walking in the evening in the mountains, Les Domaines des Courmettes, part of the Alpes Maritimes near Tourettes-Sur-Loup, you were forewarned that at certain times of the year the grey wolf could pass through. At least in Africa we had our big sticks as a deterrent. Don't expect to see many duiker (small antelope) or even a giant forest hog, as these are shy animals and probably hunted for bush meat. Buffalo and savannah elephant are now extinct in the area; the last elephant was killed in Kamiranzovu Marsh in 2000.

Enough of expectations! The reality on this current trip would be somewhat different. We stopped off on our journey through the forest, for a break and a walk at Uwinka Visitor Centre (the other is Gisakura). It had been raining incessantly for what seemed like hours, and I was not feeling particularly well, having had a tummy bug—not unusual after all the changes, flying from the UK to East Africa, in my experience. However, I was not going to miss this walk, with new friends from Lewes, Norfolk and of course with my wife as it was her first time. The walk was called the Igishigishigi (or Green) Trail, and you could really appreciate the lushness of the forest and the ambience of the vistas, from new canopy walk bridges provided by USAID. I don't suffer from vertigo and have a good head for heights, but that day, bouncing along the bridge, I learnt what the expression 'your heart is in your mouth' meant, as I looked straight ahead and talked gibberish to the one in front of me, as a coping strategy. Thankfully I spared my wife this torrent, as she was very confident up ahead. Not everyone enjoyed the experience, but we all finished and survived. From a natural history perspective, most sensible creatures were sheltering from the elements. A photographer friend was rightly bemoaning the fact that apart from a few giant invertebrates (worms and millipedes) she had nothing to take, and it was not one of the most successful trips she had been on. On our return to the visitor centre like drenched rats, I made a quick dash for the loo before re-joining the others. We heard that even those sitting all afternoon drinking coffee and going to the craft shop had allegedly seen a blue monkey *Cercopithecus mitis doggetti,* which had obligingly ambled through the trees at café and camera height.

A few days later, we had carried out the duties we came for, helping to build a house for a genocide victim, a widow and orphans. The groups that go out from the UK finance the building of the house and support the local artisans to build it, in what we know is a token gesture, but the empathy is appreciated. My wife proved a big hit, helping to entertain the local children by face painting and blowing bubbles with them, as their parents worked on the building site. Even the weather had improved as we settled into our new surroundings. The setting of our guest house, called Peace, overlooking Lake Kivu and the DRC on the other side of the lake, was beautiful with its twinkling lights reflecting off the evening lake surface. Rising in the morning at first light to the sound of fishermen singing as they return with their catch, we watched resplendent Ross's Turacos in iridescent blue plumage, yellow beak, crimson 'Mohican style' crest and outer wings, cavorting in the trees by our verandahs, in the small hours.

The first full weekend beckoned, which meant we had some down time on the Saturday morning. I had helped arrange a trip for about eight of us to visit the nearby Kingdom of Cyamudongo. These 300 hectares of Forest Park, at a slightly lower altitude (1700–2000 metres), used to be part of Nyungwe, but had become fragmented. Steps were being made to join the two forests, by landscape corridor, (the jury is still out on how successful this conservation practice is). Cyamudongo Forest, though, is known for its habituated chimps, and the rangers who track them know where they have slept overnight, and therefore where they will start the day. An early start was required to drive to the nearest forest point, before potentially a few hours of trekking. Being a morning person once I am up, I don't mind the journey, a mix of smooth metalled and bumpy off-track roads in a 4 X 4. In fact, my mind was so clear by the stimulus of the surroundings plus hopefully what was to come, I felt so much at one with my

Creator and really loved it. There was also great camaraderie with the group, engendered by a common goal. We had morning coffee, a quick breakfast and a comfort break at a place called Muyange which had a sign saying Cymudongo Tourism Promotion Cooperative (USAID). Excitement was still mounting as we heard someone on a walkie-talkie crackling intensely to the rangers, I assumed it was about the whereabouts of the apes (as it was in Kinyarwanda!). After the briefest of 'prep talks' mostly involving a big stick, we were off. The setting was stunning as the sun was just peeping above the lush tropical montane forest. We headed straight into it, going through some spectacular terrain. The outdoor educator part of me thinks, surely, we could have walked down the paths quietly, as several traversed across our more exciting 'straight as the Turaco flies' route even if it would have taken marginally longer. One year, I remembered doing the same cross-forest route, and we nearly lost a septuagenarian in a hole! I was very glad to be on hand, to help lift her out as only her head and shoulders could be seen. Respect though, for her pluck to continue undeterred — adrenalin is a wonderful thing. Chimpanzees' vocalisations reverberated around the forest, so they were heard long before they were seen. Everyone followed silently in single file: a chimp had been seen crossing the path in front, and by now the excitement was fever pitch. We had also been seen by the troupe and I suppressed my own desire to screech back at them. Suddenly in a clearing 'off piste', we slip slid into the view of a huge tree in front of us — a white fig, *Ficus exasperata* — where a large family of about ten chimps were having breakfast. We secured a position, using the sticks to steady us, as we stood in awe and wonder. The evening before, the chimps had bedded down, in smaller

94

nearby trees, to get the 'first fruits' early this morning, and we had the privilege to watch.

Don't get too close to the base of the tree! I thought, as I knew from a previous trip that, like many mammals, they like to urinate first thing in the morning, only in their case, it's from a huge tree height.

Time was flying by; cameras were clicking among many oohs and "Aah! can you see the baby one swinging?" exclaimed someone. This was for me the best sighting to date, only 20–30 minutes from the Land Rovers and I knew my photographer friend was engrossed, capturing all, using her high technology equipment. Suddenly from a side tree another troupe of monkeys could be seen passing through. These were smaller, more agile Dent's monkeys, *Cercopithecus mona denti.* They were interested in the same fruit, but they didn't want to be attacked or even killed by the larger stronger apes. They nimbly kept a safer distance and kept moving on the lighter outside branches, in a ritualistic tension these two species probably had quite often. Occasionally a dominant chimp would lash out at them with a loud scream.

A crowned hornbill was spotted in the canopy of adjacent trees, possibly eyeing up the same ripe fruit. Abruptly the Dent's monkeys all went quiet and cowered down low on the branches. I saw, out of the corner of my eye, a large bird of prey swoop over before continuing. The guide confirmed it was an African crowned eagle! So not a clear sighting by me, but all part of the morning drama in a tropical montane forest.

After about half an hour with the sun rising further, the heat and humidity was starting to take its toll on us early risers. Some chimps had started moving off, so we left those remaining to have their breakfast in peace. Walking back, tired but satisfied, I reflected — it was like a three-dimensional version of programmes from the BBC's Natural History Unit in Bristol, but with other senses stimulated too, like smell. We trundled onwards, bonded by our common experience, and thoughts turned to the rest of the day, when there was a commotion ahead! An adult male olive baboon running down the path had darted into the forest and was now perched on a tree above. As I said in the introduction, the icing on the cake of a good morning encountering wildlife in this special habitat.

21
End of sermon

You don't have to travel to the centre of Africa to have a wonderful wildlife experience, you can enjoy it just as much in 'Ole Blighty'. Try getting up in the height of summer at the crack of dawn (common theme here for any wildlife watching). Dressing gown, flip-flops (the quiet type!), hat, hot drink and just go out into the garden (if you have one), courtyard or other local beauty spot nearby and sit still. Though if it is the latter probably best to get dressed first! Magpies, jackdaws, green woodpeckers all calling, and what was that other corvid call? In my small walled garden, with flint walls on three sides and a mature hedgerow on the other, I can blend with nature. Assuming you have been using bird feeders, have a water supply or hopefully a small pond, you won't have to wait long before you also see woodpigeons and starlings nesting; three types of tits that have been habituated to me and a robin who does not social distance as he hunts in the herby rich, clover grass. Yes, that was a jay or even a family of them! What a treat that this shy most beautiful member of the crow family — with its pinkish-grey colouring and blue with black-striped wing feathers — has chosen my garden to have a drink! Two out of the three appear; the other, possibly a juvenile, is still skulking about in the trees. I only see jays in these very early morning rendezvous, but they could be there more often, when I am tucked in bed? Comparable in excitement (and every bit as challenging to photograph) as the Ross's Turaco at the Peace Guest House, Kamembe, Cyangugu in western Rwanda. A great spotted woodpecker is also a special regular visitor, making it worthwhile to keep a good supply of nuts, as they will also bring their young to educate them on easy food supplements.

For a nation that spends a fortune on what I call 'creature comforts'—feeders, bird baths, nest boxes and hogitats, plus gardens for wildlife, how come we can collectively so easily decimate their habitat? Take hedgehogs, as just one example: they need access to many gardens to roam for food, a few kilometres every night. Without a second thought, people will put down car ports, rip out garden hedges, extend patios, and put up walls, without a hedgehog-sized hole in the entrance. As I say to children in school, to make my point, hedgehogs have many skills and adaptations, but they can't pole vault! The same nation that loves reading Beatrix Potter's *Mrs Tiggywinkle* as a bedtime story, has overseen the demise of the hedgehog species as vulnerable to extinction and on the IUCN red list! We can still turn it around, but only if attitudes change dramatically and intentionally. I would suggest a more contemporary read (probably not at bedtime though for nightmares may ensue), is Pam Ayres' *The Last Hedgehog* which I have shared with many children, and it is shocking. Similarly, for other species, replacing old windows and fascia guttering with modern plastic equivalents, has a negative impact on house sparrows and martins nesting. The same can be said for converting barns that shut out barn swallows and owls. It is easy to preach about these things and I also confess, I still must follow up when my new windows were replaced, with a social nest box (x3 in one) replacement for a large house sparrow colony.

I can only deduce that this disconnection where intellectually we adore these creatures, but don't relate our practical actions to their downfall is due to a lack of education. I blatantly use every opportunity to squeeze a conservation topic into a class assembly, and the hedgehog is a perfect case study. I also know for a fact that young children really care and can influence their parents. One summer playscheme, I had it confirmed how much they care on this very topic of conservation. At the end of one day, I overheard a young girl on being picked up by her dad. When asked how it was, she implored, "We need to pick up some hedgehog food on the way home." Result!

It is encouraging that a new GCSE in Natural History is being planned for 2025 (better late than never). Conservation is complex and a multi-faceted subject, combining the biological as well as the social sciences. Sometimes hope is all we have in the face of overwhelming odds, with local and global indicators tumbling down for biodiversity while temperatures keep rising with global warming. It is challenging to feel optimistic. It is then we have to enjoy the small steps in our own garden, like bumble bees in that wild patch of stinging and non-stinging red dead nettles. Nature is resilient and will bounce back, given half a chance.

On 'my patch' during my own daily walk, I have observed Cetti's warblers slowly migrating up the valley, as they are so easy to note when they explode into song for one so small. Granted, they may be one of the few beneficiaries of climate change, with some winners but potentially more losers. I conclude with a copy of an edited post from social media 2nd

May 2020:

The day was delightful with the sun out after the rain. The sense of 'smell' is particularly enhanced in these moments, I have heard that blind people and the visually challenged relish this sense, especially heightened by their after-the-rain walks. I don't usually see whitethroats, though I know they nest further up the valley (to the north). However, with brambles migrating along the reedbeds, the habitat is changing in a way that is more suitable for not only whitethroats but also the linnets and stonechats. A displaying male whitethroat gives hope that they could nest in the future if the humble bramble trend continues.

Part 5 Au revoir —

Unexplainable encounters, accepts no fixed abode in old home, a weird winter walk and joyful Jamaica beckons in a new era, end of 2010s.

22
Postscript Poem by Seamus Heaney

And some time make the time to drive out west
Into County Clare, along the Flaggy Shore,
In September or October, when the wind
And the light, are working off each other
So that the ocean on one side is wild
With foam and glitter, and inland among stones
The surface of a slate-grey lake is lit
By the earthed lightning of a flock of swans
Their feathers roughed and ruffling, white on white,
Their fully grown headstrong-looking heads
Tucked or cresting or busy underwater.
Useless to think you'll park and capture it
More thoroughly. You are neither here nor there,
A hurry through which known and strange things pass
As big soft buffetings come at the car sideways
And catch the heart off guard and blow it open.

23

The rock from which you are hewn.
Encounters, random happenings

I am sure that encounters with wildlife move us all to a greater or lesser extent. Many people will describe these as a lovely coincidence, fate or a moment of serendipity. Some may even attribute an encounter with a wild creature as a reincarnated meeting of a deceased family member or a visit from the ancestors, depending on your religion or worldview. I know some call the butterfly the resurrection insect. As a Christian, I think of them as God incidents, as I believe God created the world and all things in it (Psalm 24 verse 1), so it is special, and we should look after it. It is certainly there to enjoy, to inspire, to keep us healthy physically, mentally and spiritually. Would I go as far as to say God times the encounters with nature? I would like to think He does, but I have no biblical theology for this, other than a faith that knows His timing is perfect in other facets of life. I would recommend a book by Peter Harris, the co-founder of A Rocha — a Christian conservation organisation — called *Kingfisher's Fire*, if you are interested in more discussion on this topic (refer to organisation notes on page 114).

I will give another example of the uncanny timing just described. You will be aware that one of several threads running through this book has been my moving from County

Antrim — old heritage home — to eventually Sussex, new home from home or geographically from the volcanic, basalt and soft water to the sedimentary chalk downlands and hard water. I was a regular visitor back to the village I grew up in, Crumlin, south Antrim, located in the Lough Neagh basin and from which it was only a couple of miles away to the west. Crumlin comes from the Irish *Cromghlinn* and means the 'Crooked Glen', referring to the heavily wooded area to which it heads, with the river running through it. The infamous Crumlin Road in Belfast is better known for its gaol and courthouse, both now reinventing themselves as tourist attractions, in the city fourteen miles to the east. My father had never lived outside the village (apart from a temporary stay in Portsmouth during the Second World War) and I always had a bed in our house, plus my brother and his wife were still active in our home church. I also had two generations of family in the adjacent churchyard! My late grandfather, whom I shared a name with, was the local Woollen Mill Manager, and the family lived in a spacious town house, right in the middle of the Main Street, in what was a wide market road. I love the story passed down from a close family friend, that the Melville family had an orchard out the back, and that the most convenient access to it, for the horse to graze at the end of the day, was straight through the house hallway! My grandfather died in 1931, leaving my grandmother with four young men mainly in their teens (one being my father), and they were rehoused in a smaller house in Lough Neagh Terrace, Mill Road, overlooking the Crumlin River (historically known as the Camlin River) and the Mill 'Brae'. The Mill Brae is unique in that it is where a rail bridge is over a road bridge which is over a river. It must have been tough for them, but I know she had a passion for Natural History, as heirloom books indicate she could take refuge in 'The wonders of nature', around the world, and of course care for her Kerry Blue terrier.

Jumping forward a whole generation, it was not until my dad was terminally ill in the winter of 2003–2004, that we realised that for the first time in many moons we would no longer have a fixed abode in the now huge village. So, my brother, one of my favourite uncles and I wondered how we could mark the occasion. Commemorative plates suddenly became appealing for the first time in my life, and we purchased two each of village landmarks like the memorial clock. Best of all, though, we spontaneously decided to walk down the Glen for a generational exchange of memories, past the spectacular waterfall to the gothic styled cockle house— folklore says it was built by a Muslim servant of the landowner to face Mecca, while others say it was a hermit's folly. Either way we used to remove a cockle, sit on a rock and throw it up behind us, into the river, making a wish before it splashed. Conversations were interrupted as we noticed dippers and grey wagtails bouncing about on the rocks above the turbulence. However, it was on our return leg, where the route narrowed steeply due to the rapid downstream of the waterfall, that we stood aghast at the sight of what looked like slightly smaller salmon leaping energetically, dashing and slipping up the rocks on their migratory route to find their spawning grounds. None of us had ever seen this before and my uncle was well into his eighties! I later researched that these were a Lough Neagh wild brown trout strain, called Dollaghan *Salmo trutta,* thought to have evolved from sea trout. Shouting and yelling above the noise of the fast-flowing water, at that moment, did a lot to lift us out of our despondency and distracted us from our current predicament.

24
Strange gates that lock in the night

T'was a week before Christmas, when nothing was stirring, that I decided to go for a walk down the local lane. It's a bit off the beaten track, not even a bridleway, but a farmer's vehicular access to his land, in the far stretches of the flattish valley of the river Ouse—south of Lewes in the South Downs National Park.

I first gained the confidence to go 'off piste', when doing the Bird Atlas 2011- 2015 for the British Trust for Ornithology and the Sussex Ornithological Society. I had a reason to walk the patch in the breeding and winter seasons. Highlights for me in the mixed fields of cereal and grazing were a woodcock, also many snipe, which are flushed out in the winter, especially in the frosty conditions, when food is scarce in the dykes around the edges. Reed, sedge and Cetti's warblers breed regularly in the spring along the reed banked two-wheel-drive pathway. It is also dear to me, as I have had close encounters over a long period of time with mammals and owls previously described, which can be observed quartering the fields.

However, this evening in the twilight, the gate was opened on a cold night. So, I proceeded with caution as hunters sometimes use the area, and you don't want to surprise them; best to wear high visibility clothing rather than camouflage. I have been too close to a shot from a high velocity rifle, shattering the wood in the copse adjacent, an experience few will have outside a war zone, such was the proximity. More likely, it would be a farm vehicle and a nodding pass would suffice, though there is always a chance a new tenant farmer will politely ask what you are doing. Caution is also always recommended as dogs are sometimes let loose and these are working dogs. On one occasion I came across hare coursing and the owners are very skittish for being observed doing a banned sport.

In the gloaming, there was nothing and still I proceeded. A vehicle from the river, one and a half miles away could return quickly. There is never really anybody walking around here as it is private land. I appreciated the crescent moon now out, a few stars were trying to peek through, as well as the odd planet. I turned to return home a few minutes later. Imagine my surprise when approaching the gate, to see it was not only shut but locked! For a split second I wondered, if maybe it had been locked all along and I had imagined it, but that was soon discounted. Obviously, no car had passed me, but who did it?

I don't believe in ghosts, so discounted the supernatural, despite being reared on stories such as those from the Emerald Isle, but it left me with a quandary. I pride myself on good field skills and can use my natural history to blend into the background, if need be. I mean if I can get close to animals in this very patch, humans would be a doddle. There is a story that indigenous African pygmies are so in tune with their forest home, that they can stand perfectly still, like statues and as the visiting human passes by they just blow on their cheek! While this frightens the living daylights out of the intruder, it is actually a very kind gesture that says, "See, I could have killed you by surprise, but decided to spare you, welcome!".

Back to the lane, so my theory is that with age, my hearing has deteriorated and maybe I did miss some clues, but my hunch (and that's all it is) is that a hunter (rarely on foot or on horseback) crossed paths unbeknown to me, possibly coming in from the side field entrances, in the few minutes I had walked up the lane. As I was on foot, they knew I could climb the gate so didn't need to acknowledge me, if they even saw me. I have never come across a walking gatekeeper before as the distances involved mean most people use vehicles. I guess some things will always remain a mystery and that is fine.

I continued homeward bound, heading towards my outside light, towards the farm hamlet with its mixed gardens, including orchards, and some remaining horse chestnut trees. A little owl could be heard scolding its solitary 'eek, eek,' knowingly, I thought, but that might be pushing anthropomorphism too far.

25
And finally — Oswald's Fish Bar, Jamaica

Of course, it is nice to visit nature reserves and national parks like Yala, Nyungwe and the South Downs, but it is special when you have an encounter that is least expected too. I had taken my wife to Ulster, to try to understand my background and heritage. She then decided to take me to see her heritage, where she was born, on the Caribbean island, of Jamaica, for mutual understanding.

After arrival in Montego Bay, we headed to the west of the island. Riu Negril was full of sun, sea, sand and jerk chicken, all good touristy things. You didn't even have to snorkel (though I did) but just stick your head under the water near the beach with a mask on, and there you could see a stingray, a giant sea slug and pipe fish! On a later visit to Kingston to see her ancestral home in Whitehall Avenue, we caught a glimpse of the island's national 'Doctor Bird' (hummingbird), or red-billed streamer-tail. The botanical gardens of any country are usually worth a visit and this one had a particularly good guide, whose mixed heritage included some Scots-Irish. A crocodile was observed in its natural habitat of mangrove swamps on a boat trip, up the Black River with a dry-humoured local guide, followed by the inevitable social media pics holding a small croc.

Extended family friends collected us for the second part of the holiday, enabling us to go to the more inaccessible places where only the locals could go—priceless. So before long, it seemed the last weekend of the holiday beckoned, and so on the Sunday morning after a Pentecostal church service in Junction, St Elizabeth, they decided to take us to St Oswald's Fish Bar at Alligator Pond.[3] As we approached the coast, the local fishermen were gutting the fish and dividing it into separate containers, the edible from the entrails. The bar was not ostentatious, as we choose our fish from the recently caught display on ice and sat down with a coconut drink at a table to enjoy the palm beach scene. It was not a swimming section of the beach, as we had done that the day before, further up the bay, besides, slim fishing boats were coming in and out in quick succession. After gutting the fish, the bucket of slop was thrown in the sea by the shallow waves. That sparked a seabird frenzy of feeding with brown pelicans *Pelecanus occidentalis* unceremoniously crash-landing into the water before gulping down the rich pickings. They were followed by the sleeker magnificent frigatebirds, *Fregata magnificens* which like masked fighter pilots with the sun behind these prehistoric looking birds, came over the palm trees and, in one fell swoop, scooped up the surface bits in a continuous, sustainable cycle. Two barking dogs were also

---

[3] The crocodile on the island is the same type as the American *Crocodylus acutus* but the confusion with the alligator is deeply ingrained in the culture since the symbol of an alligator is on the Jamaican coat of arms and a proverb saying in patois is, *"Yeah mon, nu cuss alligator long mout til yu cross di riva.* This emphasises the need for clear taxonomic identity and a Latin name over wonderful colourful local names.

entertaining us, by trying to chase the birds without getting their feet wet, but to no avail. Our spirits soared, in what for me was one of the most exciting café views for Sunday lunch—enjoy!

Quote from Colossians 1: 15 (The Message, Bible).

Christ holds it all together

We look at this Son and see God's original purpose in everything created.

Conservation Organisations

A Rocha International, 180 Piccadilly, LONDON W1 9HF, UK. +44 (0)300 770 1346 international@arocha.org www.arocha.org

A Rocha UK, 80 Windmill Road, Brentford, LONDON TW8 0QH, UK 020 8574 5935 uk@arocha.org www.arocha.org.uk
The author helped pioneer activities for children/young people access on this site https://arocha.org.uk/education-plans/

BirdWatch Ireland, Unit 20, Block D, Bullford Business Campus, Kilcoole, Greystones, Co. Wicklow, A63 RW83, Ireland. +353 (0)1 2819878 info@birdwatchireland.ie www.birdwatchireland.ie

British Trust for Ornithology, BTO, The Nunnery, Thetford, Norfolk IP24 2PU +44 (0)1842 750 info@bto.org www.bto.org

IUCN, International Union for Conservation of Nature, Cambridge Office, The David Attenborough Building, Pembroke Street, Cambridge, CB2 3QZ, UK. +44 1223 331125 www.iucn.org

Railway Land Wildlife Trust, Linklater Pavilion, Railway Lane, Lewes, BN7 2FG. 01273 477101 https://www.railwaylandproject.org/

Royal Society for the Protection of Birds, RSPB, The Lodge, Potton Road, Sandy, Bedfordshire, UK SG19 2DL. 01767 680551 www.rspb.org.uk

South Downs National Park, North Street, Midhurst, West Sussex, GU29 9DH 01730 814810 www.southdowns.gov.uk
The author has been involved in education for schools www.southdowns.gov.uk/learning/online-teacher-training/

The Wildlife Trusts, The Kiln, Mather Road, Newark, United Kingdom NG24 1WT. 01636 677711 enquiry@wildlifetrusts.org www.wildlifetrusts.org

WWF, World Wildlife Fund, WWF International Av. du Mont-Blanc 1196 Gland Switzerland +41 22 364 91 11 +41 22 364 88 36 membership@wwfus.org www.worldwildlife.org

Authors embryonic new venture: EEE, *Enriching Environmental Encounters* CIC, Lewes East Sussex. 01273-479256 davidmlvlle@gmail.com www.enrichingenvironmentalencounters.com

Artists contact details:
Carolyn Cox www.carolyncoxstudio.com and Rubi Hussey

https://www.linkedin.com/mwlite/in/rubi-h-61247419b